D1320567

07-1

DEMCO

★ ★

RHODE ISLAND

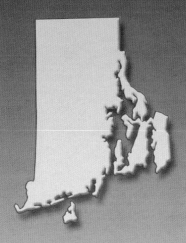

by Carol Severin

GARETH**STEVENS**
PUBLISHING
A Member of the WRC Media Family of Companies

Please visit our web site at: www.garethstevens.com
For a free color catalog describing Gareth Stevens Publishing's
list of high-quality books and multimedia programs, call
1-800-542-2595 (USA) or 1-800-387-3178 (Canada).
Gareth Stevens Publishing's fax: (414) 332-3567.

Library of Congress Cataloging-in-Publication Data

Severin, Carol.
    Rhode Island / Carol Severin.
       p. cm. — (Portraits of the states)
    Includes bibliographical references and index.
    ISBN-10: 0-8368-4707-5 — ISBN-13: 978-0-8368-4707-9 (lib. bdg.)
    ISBN-10: 0-8368-4724-5 — ISBN-13: 978-0-8368-4724-6 (softcover)
    1. Rhode Island—Juvenile literature. I. Title. II. Series.
    F79.3.S48   2007
    974.5—dc22   2006006744

This edition first published in 2007 by
Gareth Stevens Publishing
A Member of the WRC Media Family of Companies
330 West Olive Street, Suite 100
Milwaukee, WI 53212 USA

Editorial direction: Mark J. Sachner
Project manager: Jonatha A. Brown
Editor: Catherine Gardner
Art direction and design: Tammy West
Picture research: Diane Laska-Swanke
Indexer: Walter Kronenberg
Production: Jessica Morris and Robert Kraus

Picture credits: Cover, © Gibson Stock Photography; p. 4 © James P. Rowan; pp. 5, 24
© Dennis MacDonald/PhotoEdit; pp. 6, 8, 9, 11 © North Wind Picture Archives; pp. 12,
15, 16, 18, 20, 21 © Paul Rezendes/www.paulrezendes.com; p. 22 © Onne van der Wal/
CORBIS; pp. 25, 28 © AP Images; p. 26 © Susan Van Etten/PhotoEdit; p. 29 © Ezra Shaw/
Getty Images

Printed in the United States of America

1 2 3 4 5 6 7 8 9 10 09 08 07 06

CONTENTS

★ ★

Words that are defined in the Glossary appear
in **bold** the first time they are used in the text.

On the Cover: Beautiful old homes grace the harbor in Newport.
Many of these homes were built in the late 1800s.

Introduction

Welcome to Rhode Island! This small state is full of natural beauty. You can climb cliffs, watch for rare birds on islands, and explore long, sandy beaches. You can enjoy rivers, lakes, and ponds. In the forests, you may spy deer and even a black bear!

This state is full of historical sites, too. You can tour old forts and watch pretend battles. You can go to museums to learn about Native Americans and early white settlers. You can visit lighthouses and stroll through huge old homes built by very rich people.

So, enjoy Rhode Island. It is a small state that is packed with beauty, history, and fun!

The Castle Hill Lighthouse warns ships to stay away from the rocky shores of Narragansett Bay.

The state flag of Rhode Island.

RHODE ISLAND FACTS

- Became the 13th U.S. State: May 29, 1790
- Population (2004): 1,080,632
- Capital: Providence
- Biggest Cities: Providence, Warwick, Cranston, Pawtucket
- Size: 1,045 square miles (2,707 square kilometers)
- Nickname: The Ocean State
- State Tree: Red Maple
- State Flower: Violet
- State Fish: Striped Bass
- State Bird: Rhode Island Red (a type of chicken)

History

The first people to live in Rhode Island were Native Americans. They came to the area thousands of years ago. They hunted, fished, and gathered wild plants to eat. They grew squashes, pumpkins, corn, and beans, too. By the 1600s, five tribes of Natives lived here. The largest was the Narragansett tribe.

The First Europeans

The first Europeans probably reached this land in 1524. Giovanni da Verrazano was from Italy. He and his men sailed around Narragansett Bay.

In 1636, Roger Williams arrived in what is now Rhode Island.

In 1636, the first white settlement was built. It was started by a minister named Roger Williams. He believed that people should be free to think and worship as they liked. Williams had lived in the Massachusetts Bay **Colony**. Most people there did not agree with him. They sent Williams away because of his beliefs.

The Narragansetts let Williams live on their land. He made his home near the Seekonk River and named the area Providence. Soon, other settlers arrived. They wanted to be free to worship as they pleased, too. They founded Newport, Warwick, and Portsmouth.

A British Colony

In 1644, the colony of Rhode Island was formed. This new colony belonged to the British king.

Many Rhode Islanders became traders. They sold corn, lumber, fish, and wool. They also traded **molasses** and rum for slaves who were brought from Africa.

In the 1760s, the British king needed money. He saw that the people in Rhode

In 1772, angry colonists in Rhode Island burned the *Gaspee*. They were protesting British taxes.

IN RHODE ISLAND'S HISTORY

A Terrible Trade

During the 1700s, some Rhode Islanders bought and sold slaves. Slave traders paid for hundreds of trips to Africa. They brought more than one hundred thousand slaves across the ocean. The slave trade made some white people very rich. Finally, the state's leaders began to pass laws against slavery. The slave trade ended in the early 1800s.

Island and other American colonies were getting rich. He wanted a share of the wealth. So the king put taxes on goods that the colonists bought from Europe. This made the colonists angry.

The king wanted to make sure that the colonists paid the new taxes. So he sent ships and troops to guard the harbors. One of these ships was the *Gaspee*. It was **stationed** off the coast

By the mid-1800s, thousands of people had moved to Rhode Island. Many of them found work in the state's cotton mills.

of Rhode Island in 1772. One night, some Rhode Islanders rowed out to the *Gaspee*. They captured the captain and crew and set fire to the ship.

Fighting for Freedom

Many colonists wanted to be free from Britain. In 1775, they began fighting in the Revolutionary War. Many Rhode Islanders joined the fight. Rhode Island became the first colony to **declare** itself free from Britain in 1776. During the war, the British took over Newport. They burned part of the city.

After eight years of fighting, the colonists won the war. They formed the United States.

A Growing State

Rhode Island became the thirteenth U.S. state in 1790. That same year, a cotton mill was built in Pawtucket. The mill used machines to spin thread out of cotton. Soon, cotton mills sprang up in other towns. Cotton thread and cloth became the state's top products.

FACTS

A Famous Look

Ambrose Burnside lived in Rhode Island in the 1850s. He became a famous Union general during the Civil War. Burnside let his hair grow all the way down his cheeks. This unusual look became quite popular, and people named the style after him. They called this **facial** hair "side burns."

IN RHODE ISLAND'S HISTORY

Black Soldiers
The first African American army unit was formed in Rhode Island. It was called the Black Regiment, and it was formed in 1778. Each slave who joined this unit was given his freedom.

Other factories were built here, too. They made goods from silver, gold, and rubber. Providence and other cities grew as more people came to work in the factories.

The Civil War

By the mid-1800s, slavery was against the law in the state of Rhode Island and other northern states. Yet many states in the South still allowed it. Finally, these states broke away from the rest of the country. When the North tried to force the South to stay in the **Union**, war broke out.

The Civil War began in 1861. The people of Rhode Island fought for the North. Factories in the state made war supplies, too. In 1865, the North won the war. The southern states later rejoined the Union, and slavery was banned all over the country.

More Growth

After the Civil War, more factories were built. This

Near the end of the 1800s, Newport became a favorite summer vacation spot for the rich and famous.

created lots of jobs. People came from far away to work in Rhode Island factories. Many of these people came from other countries.

In the late 1800's, many rich and famous people also came to Rhode Island. They built big **mansions** and had fancy parties. They enjoyed foxhunting and **polo**.

Hard Times

By the 1920's, Rhode Island had become a costly place to do business. Many factories in the state closed down and moved to cheaper parts of the country. The **Great Depression** began in 1929. Prices for goods and crops fell all over the country. In Rhode Island, more factories closed. Many workers lost their jobs.

In 1941, the United States entered World War II. Many Rhode Islanders fought in the war. Others took jobs in factories. They made war

Today, Newport Harbor is a pretty place. Newport Bridge was built in the 1960s.

The State Today

New types of businesses have moved to the state since then. The cities are growing again. Today, the people of Rhode Island are working hard and looking forward to the future.

supplies and uniforms, and they built ships. The war made jobs for people who had been out of work.

Some of these factories closed when the war ended. Many people lost their jobs again. Some could not find work and moved away. The hard times continued for several years.

A huge hurricane hit the state in 1954. Another hurricane came the next year. Both of these storms caused terrible damage.

FACTS

Such a Long Name!

Rhode Island has a longer name than any other U.S. state. Its official name is Rhode Island and Providence Plantations. The British king gave the area this name in 1663. Rhode Island kept the name when it became a state.

1524	Giovanni da Verrazano explores Rhode Island's coast.
1636	Roger Williams founds Providence.
1644	Rhode Island becomes a British colony.
1675–1676	Colonists and local Natives fight King Philip's War.
1772	Rhode Islanders burn the *Gaspee*, a British ship.
1776–1779	British troops take over Newport and burn buildings during the Revolutionary War.
1778	First African American army unit formed in Rhode Island. Each slave who joined was given his freedom.
1790	Rhode Island becomes the thirteenth U.S. state on May 29. The first cotton mill opens in Pawtucket.
1828	Rhode Island provides money for a public school system.
1861–1865	Rhode Island sides with the North in the Civil War.
1929	The Great Depression begins. Factories close, and workers lose their jobs.
1954	Hurricane Carol hits the state and destroys millions of dollars of property. The next year, Hurricane Diane causes even more damage.

People

More than one million people live in Rhode Island. It is a huge number of people for such a small place. People live close together here. The biggest city in the state is Providence. It is also one of the biggest ports in **New England**.

A Mix of People

At first, only Native Americans made their homes here. After the British came, most of the Natives were killed. Today, less than 1 percent of the people in the state

Hispanics

This chart shows the different racial backgrounds of people in Rhode Island. In the 2000 U.S. Census, 8.7 percent of the people in Rhode Island called themselves Latino or Hispanic. Most of them or their relatives came from places where Spanish is spoken. Hispanics do not appear on this chart because they may come from any racial background.

The People of Rhode Island

Total Population 1,080,632

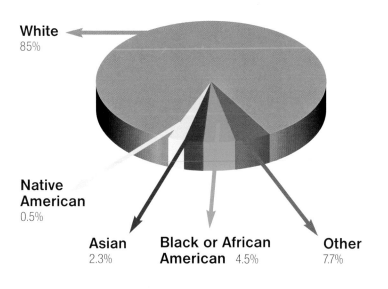

White
85%

Native
American
0.5%

Asian
2.3%

Black or African
American 4.5%

Other
7.7%

Percentages are based on the 2000 Census.

are Natives. Most of these people are Narragansetts.

During the 1700s, many Africans were brought here as slaves. When they were freed, some of them chose to make Rhode Island their home. About 5 percent of the people in the state today are black.

In the 1800s, people from Europe came to find work in factories. They came from Britain, Germany, Sweden, and other countries. Many came from Italy and Ireland, too. Today, about one out of every five people in the state trace their families to Italy. About the same number of people have Irish roots.

In more recent years, two other groups of people have moved to the state. One of these groups is Southeast Asians. They come from countries such as Cambodia and Laos. The other group is Hispanics. About 9 percent of the people in the state are Hispanic. Many of them come from South American countries.

15

Students at Brown University relax outside on a beautiful spring day. Brown is located in Providence. Its students come from all over the world.

Religion

From the start, Rhode Island has been a place for people who want to have freedom of religion and thought. Its earliest settlers from Europe were Protestant. One of the first settlers, Roger Williams, came to this area so he could worship freely. He started the first Baptist Church in the United States.

People of other faiths soon came. A small group of Jews settled in Newport. This city became home to the first Jewish **synagogue** in the United States.

Many Catholics moved here, too. Today, about one-half of the people in Rhode Island are Catholic. People of all faiths enjoy the freedom of religion that the state was built on.

Education

Rhode Island's first public school opened in Newport in 1640. For a long time, most towns could not afford schools. In 1828, the state began to give towns money to pay for schools. This helped make public schools available to most children.

Rhode Island has many colleges and universities. The oldest of them is Brown University. One of the most famous is the Rhode Island School of Design. Both of them are in Providence. The Naval War College is in Newport. The Naval Warfare Education and Training Center also is in Newport.

Famous People of Rhode Island

Anne Hutchinson

Born: June or July 1591, Alford, England

Died: August or September 1643, New York, New York

Anne Hutchinson was a religious leader. During the 1630s, she lived in the Massachusetts Bay Colony. There, women were expected to be quiet and do as the leaders of the colony said. Yet Hutchinson spoke out. She said the leaders of the colony were wrong about some things. Many people agreed with her, but the colony's leaders did not. They forced her to leave. She moved to Rhode Island so she could worship in her own way. Others went with her. Together, this group of people founded the city of Portsmouth.

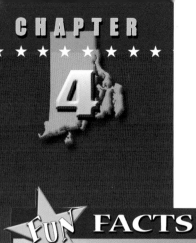

The Land

Rhode Island is on the Atlantic Coast, in the northeastern part of the nation. It is the smallest U.S. state. It is about 40 miles (64 km) from east to west, and 47 miles (76 km) from north to south. Winters are quite cool here and summers are warm but not hot.

Lay of the Land

The state is shaped like a rectangle. A large bay with islands stretches from the ocean into the southeastern part of the state. The land near the bay is called the Coastal Lowlands. The hilly land in the northwest is called the New England Upland.

The Coastal Lowlands

The eastern one-third of Rhode Island makes up the Coastal Lowlands. This

On Block Island, sandy dunes stretch down to the ocean shore.

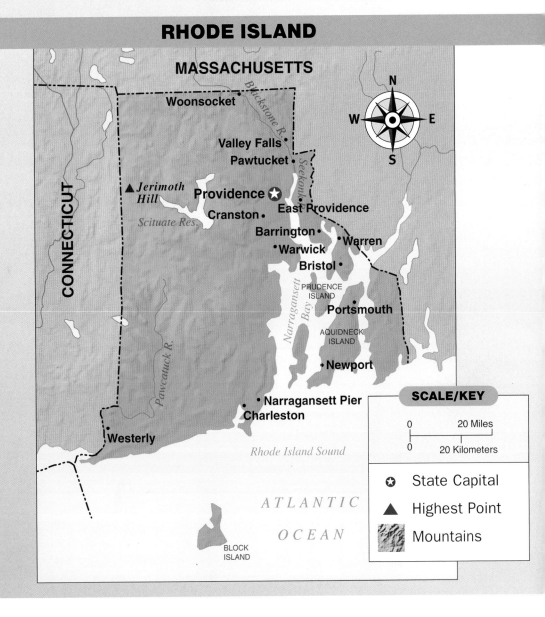

MASSACHUSETTS

Woonsocket

Blackstone R.

Valley Falls •
Pawtucket •

Seekonk R.

CONNECTICUT

▲ *Jerimoth Hill*

Providence ✪

Scituate Res.

Cranston •

East Providence

Barrington •

• Warren

• Warwick

Bristol •

Narragansett Bay

PRUDENCE ISLAND

Portsmouth

AQUIDNECK ISLAND

• Newport

Pawcatuck R.

• Narragansett Pier

Charleston

Westerly

Rhode Island Sound

ATLANTIC

OCEAN

BLOCK ISLAND

SCALE/KEY

0   20 Miles

0   20 Kilometers

✪ State Capital

▲ Highest Point

Mountains

area is on a low sandy **plain** that stretches down to the ocean. Along the coast lie 40 miles (64 km) of sandy beaches. Narragansett Bay cuts deep into the lowlands.

It is 26 miles (42 km) long. Lagoons, salt marshes, and beaches surround the bay.

The state includes about thirty islands. Many of them

are in Narragansett Bay. The biggest island in the bay is Aquidneck. It is sometimes called Rhode Island, just like the state. The biggest island off the coast is Block Island. It lies in the ocean, about 7 miles (11 km) from shore.

The New England Upland

The northwestern two-thirds of the state is called the New England Upland. This land has steep hills and cliffs. It is higher than the rest of the state. Jerimoth Hill is the highest point in the state. It is 812 feet (247 meters) high. Forests cover much of the land.

Rivers and creeks wind

Major Rivers
Blackstone River 40 miles (64 km) long
Pawtuxet River 28 miles (45 km) long
Pawcatuck River 23 miles (37 km) long

through this region. They flow toward the bay and the ocean. In some places, they plunge down cliffs. This creates beautiful waterfalls.

Rhode Island has only small lakes. The biggest one was man-made. It is

The Rose Island Lighthouse stands guard on the shores of Narragansett Bay.

the Scituate Reservoir. This lake was created by a dam on the Pawtuxet River. The lake provides fresh water for about one-half of the people in the state.

Plants and Animals

More than fifty types of trees grow in Rhode Island. They include oak, beech, cedar, elm, pine, and maple. Many of these trees have leaves that change colors in the autumn. The state tree is the red maple. Its leaves turn bright red in the fall.

The state has lots of white-tailed deer. Smaller animals include red foxes, coyotes, and minks. Raccoons, squirrels, and woodchucks also live in Rhode Island. Many kinds of fish swim in the waters of the state.

Rhode Island's Birds

Rhode Island is home to about three hundred types of birds. Ducks, herons, geese, and terns are seen near the coast. Red-tailed hawks, osprey, blue jays, and robins are found inland. Wild turkeys live in the west. Block Island is home to dozens of kinds of rare birds.

Autumn is a beautiful time of year in Rhode Island. Here, red maples line a quiet pond in the town of West Greenwich.

Economy

Many of the early white settlers in Rhode Island were fishermen and farmers. Others built ships and shipped goods. Today, some people still fish for a living. They catch lobsters, flounders, clams, squids, and scallops. Other people still build ships and ship goods. But less than 1 percent of the state's money now comes from farming. The state has fewer than one thousand farms.

Making Goods

The first factories were built here in the late 1700s. Now, many Rhode Islanders work in factories. They make clothes, toys, electronics, and jewelry. Some turn metal into parts for machines or buildings.

These fishermen are spreading a fishing net. They are working off the coast of Rhode Island.

Providing Services

In Rhode Island, thousands of people have service jobs. Service workers help other people. Teachers, lawyers, and doctors are all service workers. The state is well known for health services. Rhode Island has many hospitals and big medical centers. It is home to big insurance and real estate companies, too.

Helping Tourists

Millions of people visit Rhode Island each year. They come to enjoy the state's sandy beaches, towns and cities, and historic sites. These visitors spend money at hotels and restaurants. Many workers are needed to run these tourist businesses. Like doctors and lawyers, these people are service workers.

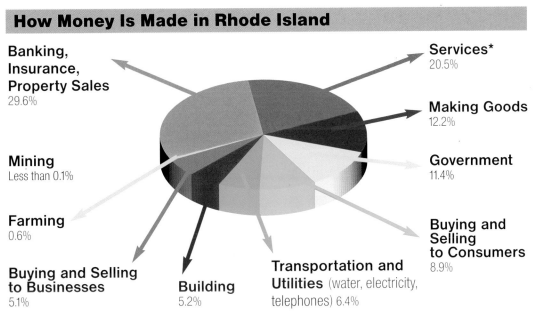

How Money Is Made in Rhode Island

Banking, Insurance, Property Sales
29.6%

Services*
20.5%

Making Goods
12.2%

Mining
Less than 0.1%

Government
11.4%

Farming
0.6%

Buying and Selling to Consumers
8.9%

Buying and Selling to Businesses
5.1%

Building
5.2%

Transportation and Utilities (water, electricity, telephones) 6.4%

* Services include jobs in hotels, restaurants, auto repair, medicine, teaching, and entertainment.

Government

Providence is the capital of Rhode Island. The leaders of the state work there. The state government has three parts. They are the executive, legislative, and judicial branches.

Executive Branch

The executive branch makes sure state laws are carried out. The leader of the executive branch is the governor. The lieutenant governor is second in command.

Rhode Island's capitol building was built in the late 1890s. The building is known as the State House.

State representatives recite the Pledge of Allegiance. Their meetings are held in the House Chamber at the State House.

Legislative Branch

The legislature is called the General Assembly. It has two parts. They are the Senate and the House of Representatives. These groups work together to make state laws.

Judicial Branch

Judges and courts make up the judicial branch. They may decide whether people who have been **accused of** committing crimes are guilty.

Local Governments

Rhode Island has thirty-nine towns and cities. Each has its own government. Most towns and cities are run by a team of people. They are led by a council and either a mayor or a city manager.

RHODE ISLAND'S STATE GOVERNMENT

Executive		Legislative		Judicial	
Office	**Length of Term**	**Body**	**Length of Term**	**Court**	**Length of Term**
Governor	4 years	Senate (50 members)	2 years	Supreme (5 justices)	Life
Lieutenant Governor	4 years	House of Representatives (100 members)	2 years	Superior (22 judges)	Life

Things to See and Do

If you like to go to the beach, you will love Rhode Island! East Beach is in Charlestown. It has white sand, grassy **dunes**, and blue-green water. First Beach in Newport is a great spot for surfing and windsurfing. Block Island is known for its fine beaches, too.

Historic Sites and Museums

This state is filled with historic places. In Pawtucket, you can visit the Slater Mill Historical Site. It is a good place to learn about the first water-powered cotton mill in the United States. In Portsmouth,

Swimmers and sunbathers enjoy a day at the beach in Narragansett.

FACTS

Summer Cottage

One of the fanciest mansions in Newport is the Breakers. This home was built in 1895 for a rich family named Vanderbilt. The Vanderbilts called it a "summer cottage." This makes it sound small, but it is not. The Breakers has seventy rooms. It is much more like a castle than a cottage. Like many of the mansions in Newport, it is now a National Historic Landmark.

Nathanael Greene

Born: August 17, 1742, Warwick, Rhode Island

Died: June 19, 1786, Savannah, Georgia

Nathanael Greene grew up in Rhode Island. During the Revolutionary War, he fought against the British and won many important battles. Late in the war, he was put in charge of the armed forces in the south. This made him second only to General George Washington. Today, Greene is remembered as a hero. He was one of the greatest leaders of the Revolutionary War.

you can visit Butts Hill Fort. A Revolutionary War battle was fought there more than two hundred years ago.

Providence is home to fine museums. The Providence Children's Museum is lots of fun. You can explore a cave, climb a tree, and build your own fountain. In Newport, you can go to a doll museum and a museum about boats. You can also see many grand old mansions.

Festivals

Warwick holds a festival in June, called "*Gaspee* Days." This event celebrates the burning of a British ship before the Revolutionary War. It includes a pretend battle and a parade.

In Providence, you can see a nighttime sight called WaterFire. It takes place several times a month, from spring through fall. Dozens of bonfires are lit on the rivers that run through the city. From sunset until late at night, flickering flames light up the walkways and parks nearby.

Sports

The state has three minor-league sports teams. The Pawtucket Red Sox play baseball. The Providence

Flying Horses

The Flying Horse Carousel is the oldest merry-go-round in the United States. It was built in Westerly in 1867. On this carousel, the horses hang on chains. When the carousel whirls around, the riders feel like they are almost flying!

The JVC Jazz Festival-Newport is the oldest outdoor jazz festival in the United States. Each year, this three-day festival draws huge crowds from near and far.

Famous People of Rhode Island

Lizzie Murphy

Born: April 13, 1894, Warren, Rhode Island

Died: July 27, 1964, place unknown

Lizzie Murphy was the first woman to play major-league baseball. Her friends called her "Spike." She began playing for **amateur** teams when she was a teenager. She joined a team called the Boston All-Stars when she was twenty-four years old. She played first base from 1918 to 1935. She was so good that she played in two all-star games in the 1920s. Her fans called her the "Queen of Baseball."

International tennis events are still held at the Tennis Hall of Fame in Newport.

Bruins play hockey. In East Providence, fans cheer for the Rhode Island Stingrays soccer team.

Newport is famous for the sports of sailing and tennis. The famous America's Cup sailing race was held here for many years. Today, the city is home to the America's Cup Hall of Fame. Also in Newport is the International Tennis Hall of Fame. The oldest grass tennis courts in the country are in this city.

GLOSSARY

accused of — blamed for

amateur — someone who plays sports but is not paid for playing

colony — a group of people living in a new land but controlled by the place they came from

declare — to say in a strong way

dunes — hills of sand that have been created by wind

facial — having to do with the face

Great Depression — a time, in the 1930s, when many people lost jobs and businesses lost money

mansions — very large, expensive homes

molasses — a sweet syrup made when sugarcane is processed into sugar

New England — a part of the northeastern United States made up of six states: Maine, Vermont, New Hampshire, Rhode Island, Massachusetts, and Connecticut

plain — a large area of flat or rolling land that has few trees

polo — a ball game played on horseback.

reclaim — to take back something that once was yours

salt marshes — a low area of land sometimes flooded with ocean water

stationed — put in a place

synagogue — a place where Jews worship

Union — the United States

Books

Finding Providence: The Story of Roger Williams. I Can Read (series). Avi (HarperTrophy)

R is for Rhode Island Red: A Rhode Island Alphabet. Discover America State by State (series). Mark R. Allio (Sleeping Bear Press)

The Rhode Island Colony. Spirit of America (series). Barbara A. Somervill (The Child's World)

Rhode Island Facts and Symbols. The States and Their Symbols (series). Kathy Feeney (Capstone Press)

Thunder from the Clear Sky. Marcia Sewall (Atheneum)

Web Sites

Enchanted Learning: Rhode Island
www.enchantedlearning.com/usa/states/rhodeisland/

Kidspace @ The Internet Public Library: Rhode Island
www.ipl.org/div/kidspace/stateknow/ri1.html

Rhode Island Facts and Trivia
www.50states.com/facts/rdisl.htm

Science of Baseball: Lizzie Murphy
www.exploratorium.edu/baseball/murphy.html

INDEX